Ducklings
on the Run

Abby Summerhill and Noni (Gail) Summerhill
Illustrated by Alyssa Mazon

Ducklings on the Run

Copyright, 2019
Abby Summerhill and Noni Summerhill

Illustrations, Copyright 2019
Alyssa Mazon

No text or images in this book
may be used or reproduced in any
manner without written permission
of the copyright holders.

All Rights Reserved

Cover layout and interior pages
layout by Capri Porter.

Printed in the United States of America

ISBN: 978-1-7322135-7-9

Published by
Legacies & Memories
St. Augustine, Florida

www.LegaciesandMemoriesPublishing.com

This Book Belongs To

_____

I like spending time with Noni, my grandma.
We always have fun.
In the alley behind our family's townhouse, I make her a seat out of my brother's baseball bucket.

Noni will wait for me while I ride
my scooter around the block.

When I am almost back to our townhouse, Noni motions for me to come quickly and quietly. She wants me to see something that's very unusual.

It's a mama duck beside the gutter on the balcony above the garage of our neighbor's townhouse.

She is squawking and making lots of noise.
Suddenly, she flies to the ground.
A moment later, we see a duckling fall out of the downspout. It doesn't appear to be hurt.

Mama duck appears to be upset.
She begins pacing back and forth.
The baby is following closely.

Mama duck's squawking is so loud that people in nearby townhouses are coming onto their balconies.

Two girls tell us there is a nest with ducklings on the balcony of the townhouse where the mother duck had been.

The girls climb from their balcony
and walk to the nest.
They discover four ducklings
in a flower planter.

Now we understand why she is so upset!
She doesn't know how to get her
baby back into the nest on the balcony.

The girls walk to the fire station around
the corner to see if they can
find someone to help.

A few moments later, a police car
drives through the alley.
My Noni thinks police have come to the rescue.

"What ducks?" asks the policeman.
He tells us he's not here to rescue ducks.
He says he's sorry he can't help.

By now, several people have arrived
to see what's happening —
and discuss what can be done.

The two girls come back from
the fire station. They get a box and
again climb onto the balcony.

With gloves on their hands,
they carefully pick up the babies
and put them in the box.

They bring the box to the front of the house,
which is shaded by trees.
They put the box on the ground.
During all this time,
mama duck is squawking loudly.

As soon as she hears the ducklings calling, she runs to the babies. The little one from the downspout runs as fast as it can to keep up with its mother.

Mama duck is not able to get
the babies out of the box.
So, the girls tip it over.
The little ones come tumbling out.

Mama and her five ducklings are together again!

She and her babies waddle off
to nearby woods and a stream.
We follow and try to find them,
but she is too good at hiding them.

The next day,
Noni and I walk to the stream.
We see a mother duck and five ducklings.
They are swimming happily.